Joe Mauer

Revised Edition

By Jeffrey Zuehlke

AMAZING ATHLETES

Lerner Publications Company • Minneapolis

For Graham, Saint Paul kid; and for Jon Fishman, the greatest left-handed-hitting editor ever

Lerner Publications Company
A division of Lerner Publishing Group, Inc.
241 First Avenue North
Minneapolis, MN 55401 U.S.A.

Website address: www.lernerbooks.com

Library of Congress Cataloging-in-Publication Data

Zuehlke, Jeffrey, 1968–
    Joe Mauer / by Jeffrey Zuehlke. — Rev. ed.
      p.   cm. — (Amazing athletes)
    Includes bibliographical references and index.
    ISBN 978–0–7613–7066–6 (lib. bdg. : alk. paper)
    1. Mauer, Joe, 1983-—Juvenile literature. 2. Baseball players—United States—Biography—Juvenile literature. 3. Minnesota Twins (Baseball team)—Biography—Juvenile literature. I. Title.
GV865.M376Z84 2011
796.357092—dc22 [B]   2010036004

Manufactured in the United States of America
1 – BP – 12/31/10

TABLE OF CONTENTS

Joe Mauer watches the ball sail into the outfield.

HOME SWEET HOME

Minnesota Twins' **catcher** Joe Mauer swung at the pitch. Crack! The ball flew into the outfield. Joe ran to second base with a **double** as teammate Nick Punto scored. The Twins were leading the Boston Red Sox, 3–0.

Twins fans are used to seeing Joe on the bases. In 2009 he won the **batting title** for the **American League (AL)**. Joe was also named the league's **Most Valuable Player (MVP)** that year. But this 2010 game against the Red Sox was special for Joe and the Twins. It was the first **regular season** game at Target Field, the Twins new outdoor ballpark.

Joe is the only AL catcher to win the batting title. He took the title for the first time in 2006. Then he won batting titles again in 2008 and 2009.

Fans cheer on the Twins during the first game at the new Target Field in Minneapolis, Minnesota.

The Twins played their home games at the Hubert H. Humphrey Metrodome (later renamed Mall of America Field) for 28 seasons. The team and its fans were glad to have a brand new place to play beginning in 2010. "I know people here have been waiting a long time for this," Joe said. "It's definitely a special place and I'm glad it's here."

Joe came to bat again in the fourth inning. He swung hard and hit a **single**. Teammate Denard Span ran home to score. The Twins had the lead, 4–1.

The teams didn't score again until the seventh inning. Joe's teammate Jason Kubel hit a ball high into the sky. It sailed up and over the wall in right field. It was the first **home run** ever hit at Target Field! The crowd roared. "I'll remember it for the rest of my life," Kubel said after the game.

Jason Kubel stands at home plate after hitting the first home run at Target Field.

The Red Sox scored their second run in the eighth inning. But they couldn't catch the Twins. Minnesota won the game, 5–2.

The fans at the game were very excited about the new ballpark. But they saved their biggest cheers for Joe. "When they announced my name, the fans were pumped. You could tell," Joe said later. "I was glad we got the win."

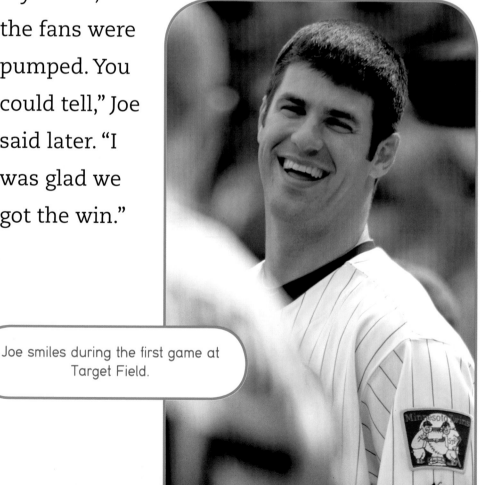

Joe smiles during the first game at Target Field.

Saint Paul is the capital of Minnesota. It is across the Mississippi River from Minneapolis, the home of the Twins.

NOT YOUR AVERAGE JOE

Joseph Patrick Mauer was born on April 19, 1983, in Saint Paul, Minnesota. He was born into a family of talented athletes. His father, uncles, and older brothers were all good at sports.

From an early age, Joe loved baseball. "I guess as soon as I picked up a bat [at the age of two], I didn't let go," says Joe. Even as a small kid, he showed talent. In fact, he was kicked off his local T-ball team because he was too good. "They wanted me out of the league because I hit the ball too hard," says Joe.

Joe grew up in Saint Paul. Like many Minnesota kids, he was a big fan of the Twins. Twins legend Kirby Puckett was his favorite player. Joe dreamed of playing for his hometown team.

Kirby Puckett is one of the most popular players in Twins history.

As a kid, Joe spent much of his free time playing sports. He was good at football and basketball. But baseball was his favorite sport. He and his older brothers played stickball on the street in front of their house. "We'd get out there with a broom handle and tennis ball and play," says Joe.

The hitting tool that Joe's dad made was so successful that the Mauers decided to sell it to the public. The Mauer Quick Swing is one of the most popular hitting tools on the market.

Joe's dad invented a special tool to help his boys practice their hitting. It was a V-shaped pipe on a stand. The batter dropped a ball into one end of the pipe. The ball rolled out the other end. The batter swung at the ball as it came out. The boys used it to practice for hours and hours.

Joe's dad, Jake Mauer II *(right)*, stands with his father, Jake Mauer I. Joe's dad spent many years coaching his sons' teams.

The tool helped Joe perfect his swing. "He'd bring it into the gym three or four times a week," said one of his baseball coaches. "And the other kids couldn't come close using baseballs and bats. Meanwhile, Joe was hitting golf balls with a piece of pipe."

Joe keeps his eye on the ball as he bats for his high school team, the Cretin-Derham Hall Raiders.

THREE-SPORT STAR

By the time he reached high school, everyone could see that Joe had special talent. It looked as if he had a future as a pro athlete. But Joe was a star in football, basketball, and baseball. Which sport would he choose?

By his **sophomore** year, he was getting a lot of attention from pro baseball teams. "We had

been tracking him since he was about fifteen," said then Twins general manager Terry Ryan. "Left-handed hitting catchers are tough to come [by]. And there's no question that Joe was talented."

Joe went to the same high school as MLB Hall of Fame player Paul Molitor.

Meanwhile, Joe was the best player on his basketball team too. For his **junior** and **senior** seasons, he was named All-State in basketball. But he was an even better football player. As the star **quarterback**, Joe led his Cretin-Derham Hall Raiders team to two state championship games. The Raiders won the title in Joe's junior season in 1999.

The team lost the title game in 2000. But Joe still had a spectacular season. He threw for more than 3,000 yards. He also threw 41 touchdown passes. Joe even set a state record with seven touchdown passes in one game.

Joe ended his high school football career as the top player in the country. He was named the 2000 High School Football Player of the Year. Joe was even named as a star of the future in *Sports Illustrated* magazine.

Joe gets ready to make a throw as quarterback for his high school team.

All the top colleges wanted him to play quarterback for them. He got calls from the University of Miami, the University of Michigan, and other schools.

Joe wasn't sure what he wanted to do. He still had a season of high school baseball to play. But if he wanted to play college football, he had to make a decision. Joe signed a letter to play for the Florida State Seminoles. But he could change his mind later.

Joe's last high school baseball season was just as good as his football season. **Scouts** from pro

Joe struck out only once in his entire high school baseball career. "It was junior year, and it was in the state tournament. I came back to the bench and everybody thought something was wrong with me."

Joe played catcher on his high school baseball team.

baseball teams watched all of his games. "I just remember coming out of the locker room and you'd see all these scouts over there," said Joe. "Every team represented, almost every day."

At the end of the season, he was named the top high school baseball player in the country. No athlete had ever been named the best baseball and football player before.

So what would Joe do? Would he play football or baseball? He wasn't totally sure.

Joe puts on a Twins jersey after being picked first in the **Major League Baseball (MLB)** draft on June 5, 2001.

WHERE WILL JOE GO?

Meanwhile, the Major League Baseball **draft** was coming up in June 2001. All the teams would be selecting players.

Deep down, Joe wanted to play baseball. He decided that if a team made him a top pick, he would play baseball. To make things more exciting, the Minnesota Twins had the first pick in the draft that year.

When draft day came, the Twins took Joe with the first pick. "It was just an unbelievable feeling," he said.

"Everything worked out perfectly," said Joe's older brother Bill. "Joe wanted to be a Twin. He didn't want to go anywhere else. The Twins are his team."

Like most players, Joe started his pro career in the **minor leagues**. His first team was the Elizabethton Twins of the Appalachian League. He moved to Tennessee, far away from home. Luckily, he already knew one of his teammates. The Twins had drafted his brother Jake that same summer. Both played for Elizabethton in 2001.

Joe's first season was amazing. His **batting average** was an incredible .400! He was named the league's top **prospect**.

By his third year as a pro, Joe was ready for the big leagues. He began the 2004 season as the Twins' starting catcher. He was just 21 years old.

Joe's fans hold up a banner for his major-league debut on April 5, 2004.

Joe got a hit on the first day. He looked set to have a good season, but he hurt his knee two days later. The knee took a long time to heal. Joe ended up playing in just 35 games.

He came into 2005 healthy and ready to

play. He had a strong season. Joe played in 131 games. He finished with a team-best .294 batting average and 26 doubles.

By this time, Joe was already one of the Twins' most popular players. Fans loved his great hitting and his humble attitude. "He's just a good baseball player," says his manager, Ron Gardenhire. "He's . . . a good combination of a person and a player."

Joe tags out Kansas City Royals player Emil Brown at home plate in 2006.

CATCHING HISTORY

There is a reason why so few catchers have won batting titles. Catchers get hit with foul balls and wild pitches. All the aches and pains make it hard to hit well.

Playing catcher is tough, but Joe was ready to take it to the next level in 2006. He hit .316

in the first month of the season. Then Joe's hitting really took off. He batted .386 in May. He hit for an unbelievable .452 average in June! The Twins won the AL **Central Division** title by one game.

Minnesota lost to the Oakland A's in the first round of the **playoffs**. But it was a great season. Joe won the batting title with a .347 average. First baseman Justin Morneau was named AL MVP. Superstar pitcher Johan Santana won the AL **Cy Young Award**.

Joe hands the ball to pitcher Johan Santana during a game in 2006.

When the 2007 season started, the Twins struggled. Joe missed a lot of games because of injuries. The Cleveland Indians won the AL Central.

The Twins traded Santana to the New York Mets before the start of the 2008 season. The team played well without their star pitcher. Joe won his second AL batting title with a

Joe gets a hit during a game against the Detroit Tigers in 2008.

In 2008, Joe became the first Twins catcher to start an All-Star Game. He also started the game for the AL in 2009 and 2010.

.328 average. Morneau finished second in the AL with 129 **runs batted in (RBI)**.

But the Twins couldn't shake the Chicago White Sox. After 162 regular season games, the two teams both had 88 victories. They had to play a final game to see who would win the AL Central. Minnesota played well, but the White Sox won the game, 1–0. "We're going home and they're going to the playoffs," Morneau said after the loss. "It's going to hurt for awhile."

Joe missed the beginning of the 2009 season with a sore back. He returned with a bang on May 1 against the Kansas City Royals. In his first **at-bat** of the season, Joe sent the ball over the outfield fence for a home run!

The home run was a sign of things to come. Joe would end the season with 28 home runs. He also finished with an amazing .365 batting average. That was good enough to win his third AL batting title. Joe was also named the AL MVP. Best of all, the Twins won the AL Central. The season came to an end in the first round of the playoffs against the New York Yankees.

Minnesota realized that Joe is a special player. In 2010, the team signed him to a huge contract worth $184 million. Joe quickly went out and proved that the money was well spent. He hit .327 for the year and led Minnesota to the AL Central title. But their season ended with another first-round playoff loss to the Yankees.

The Twins are very glad to have their hometown hero on the team. With Joe behind the plate, the team's future is bright.

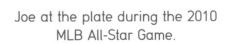

Joe at the plate during the 2010 MLB All-Star Game.

Selected Career Highlights

2010 Signed an eight-year, $184 million contract with the Twins
Finished third in batting in the American League with a .327 average

2009 Voted the American League's Most Valuable Player
Won the American League batting title with a .365 average

2008 Won the American League batting title with a .328 average
Became first Twins catcher to start the All-Star Game

2007 Signed a four-year, $33 million contract with the Twins

2006 Became the first AL catcher to win the batting title, with a .347 average
Named AL Player of the Month for June
Named to first MLB All-Star Game

2005 Had 144 hits in 131 games for a .294 batting average
Had a 9-game hitting streak and an 8-game hitting streak

2004 Played in his first MLB game
Got his first MLB hit in his first MLB game

2003 Played for the Fort Myers Miracle and the New Britain Rock Cats in the minor leagues
Finished the season with a .338 batting average—best among all minor-league catchers
Named Minor League Player of the Year by *Baseball America*
Ranked best prospect in the Eastern League and Florida State League

2002 Played for the Quad City River Bandits in the Midwest League
Selected to the Midwest League All-Star Team

2001 First player taken in the 2001 MLB draft
Hit .400 in first minor-league season for the Elizabethton Twins
Named top catching prospect in baseball by *Baseball America* magazine

Glossary

American League (AL): one of MLB's two leagues. The American League has 14 teams, including the Minnesota Twins, New York Yankees, Boston Red Sox, Detroit Tigers, Chicago White Sox, and others.

at-bat: a chance to hit at home plate

batting average: a statistic that judges a player's success at hitting the ball. For example, if a hitter gets 3 hits in 10 at-bats, the batting average would be .300.

batting title: an award that goes to the hitter with the best batting average in the league at the end of the regular season

catcher: a position in baseball. The catcher squats behind the plate and catches pitches. The catcher also helps the pitcher choose which pitches to throw and is responsible for throwing out base runners who are trying to steal bases.

Central Division: one of the three groups that make up the American League. The AL Central is made up of the Chicago White Sox, Cleveland Indians, Detroit Tigers, Kansas City Royals, and Minnesota Twins.

Cy Young Award: an award given out each year to the best pitcher in each of the major leagues

double: a hit in which the batter is able to reach second base safely

draft: a yearly event in which teams take turns selecting players from a group

home run: a hit that allows the batter to circle all the bases to score a run

junior: a third-year high school or college student

Major League Baseball (MLB): the top group of professional men's baseball teams in North America. MLB is divided into the National League and the American League.

minor leagues: groups of teams in which players improve their skills and prepare to move to the majors

Most Valuable Player (MVP): an award given out each year to the best player in each of the major leagues

playoffs: a series of games played after the regular season to determine a championship

prospect: a player experts believe will be a good MLB player

quarterback: a position in football whose main job is to lead the offense and throw passes

regular season: the regular schedule for a season. Each MLB team plays 162 regular season games. The top eight teams go to the playoffs.

runs batted in (RBI): the number of runners able to score on a batter's hit or walk

scouts: people whose job it is to watch players and judge their talent and skills

senior: a fourth-year high school or college student

single: a hit in which the batter is able to reach first base safely

sophomore: a second-year high school or college student

Further Reading & Websites

Briand, Kevin. *The Baseball Book: A Young Player's Guide to Baseball.* Richmond Hills, ONT: Firefly Books, 2003.

Donovan, Sandy. *Derek Jeter*. Minneapolis: Lerner Publications Company, 2004.

Kelly, James. *Baseball*. New York: DK Publishing, 2005.

Kennedy, Mike, and Mark Stewart. *Long Ball: The Legend and Lore of the Home Run*. Minneapolis: Millbrook Press, 2006.

Zuehlke, Jeffrey. *Johan Santana*. Minneapolis: Lerner Publications Company, 2007.

Joe Mauer Fan Club
http://www.joemauerfanclub.com
Learn more about Joe and his great career from his fan club site.

Joe Mauer's Quick Swing Batting Aids
http://www.mauersquickswing.com
Learn more about the tool that Joe used to become a great hitter.

Minnesota Twins: The Official Site
http://minnesota.twins.mlb.com
The Minnesota Twins official site has all the latest news about the Twins and Joe Mauer.

Official MLB site
http://www.mlb.com
The official site of Major League Baseball provides up-to-date news and statistics of all 30 major-league teams and every major-league player.

Sports Illustrated Kids
http://www.sikids.com
The *Sports Illustrated Kids* website covers all sports, including baseball.

Index

Photo Acknowledgments

The images in this book are used with the permission of: © Eric Miller/Reuters/CORBIS, p. 4; © Rich Pilling/MLB Photos via Getty Images, p. 6; © Hannah Foslien/Getty Images, pp. 7, 8; © Steve Dahlman/SuperStock, p. 9; AP Photo/Jim Mone, pp. 10, 18, 20; © Carlos Gonzalez/*Minneapolis Star Tribune*/ZUMA Press, p. 12; © Vince Muzik/Icon SMI, pp. 13, 17; © Dawn Villella/*St. Paul Pioneer Press*, p. 15; AP Photo/Ed Zurga, p. 22; AP Photo/Charlie Riedel, p. 23; © Leon Halip/US Presswire, p. 24; © Josh Holmberg/Cal Sport Media/Zuma Press/Icon SMI, p. 26; © Paul Buck/epa/CORBIS, p. 27; © Ron Vesely/Getty Images, p. 28.

Front Cover: © Ron Vesely/Getty Images.